LEARN TO READ ARABIC

HAUGAN SCHOOL
4540 N. HAMLIN AVE.
CHICAGO, ILL. 60625

ESEA TITLE VII BILINGUAL FUNDS

Learn to Read Arabic

RAJA T. NASR
M. A., Ed. D., F. I. B. A., F. R. S. A.
Professor of Education and Linguistics
Beirut University College
Beirut, Lebanon

LIBRAIRIE DU LIBAN
Riad Solh Square
Beirut, Lebanon

INTERNATIONAL BOOK CENTRE
P. O. Box #295
Troy, Michigan 48099, U.S.A.

© RAJA T. NASR, 1978
First Published 1978
ISBN 0-917062-02-7

FOREWORD

The teaching of foreign languages has, in recent years, gone through radical changes due to the revealing findings of modern linguistic science. Among the linguistic principles involved in teaching foreign languages, three stand out as basic:
1. that language is primarily oral,
2. that the problems encountered in learning a foreign language stem primarily from the learner's native language, and
3. that to master a foreign language, the learner should establish new habits of its phonological and grammatical patterns through constant drill and repetition, preferably with a native speaker.

LEARN TO READ ARABIC is designed to give learners of Arabic as a foreign language a concise presentation of the Arabic alphabet and writing system, as well as beginning drills in reading and pronunciation. The approach is especially adapted for learners whose native language is English.

In addition to learning how to read Arabic, this self-taught course should also:
1. give you ample practice in the recognition and production of all the Standard Arabic sounds;
2. familiarize you with a basic vocabulary;
3. acquaint you with basic grammatical structures.

To benefit from this material, read the entire text carefully first; then follow the instructions given with reference to the taped materials. Repeat different parts and exercises (especially 1-7) as needed.

CONTENTS

Foreword

Contents

Diagram of the Vocal Apparatus

1. The Consonants ....page 1
2. The Vowels 3
3. Arabic Writing 4
4. Velarization 8
5. Length 9
6. Stress 10
7. Intonation 11
8. The Definite Article 12
9. Exercises - Words 14
10. General Exercises 18

Bibliography by the Same Author .. 39

DIAGRAM OF THE VOCAL APPARATUS

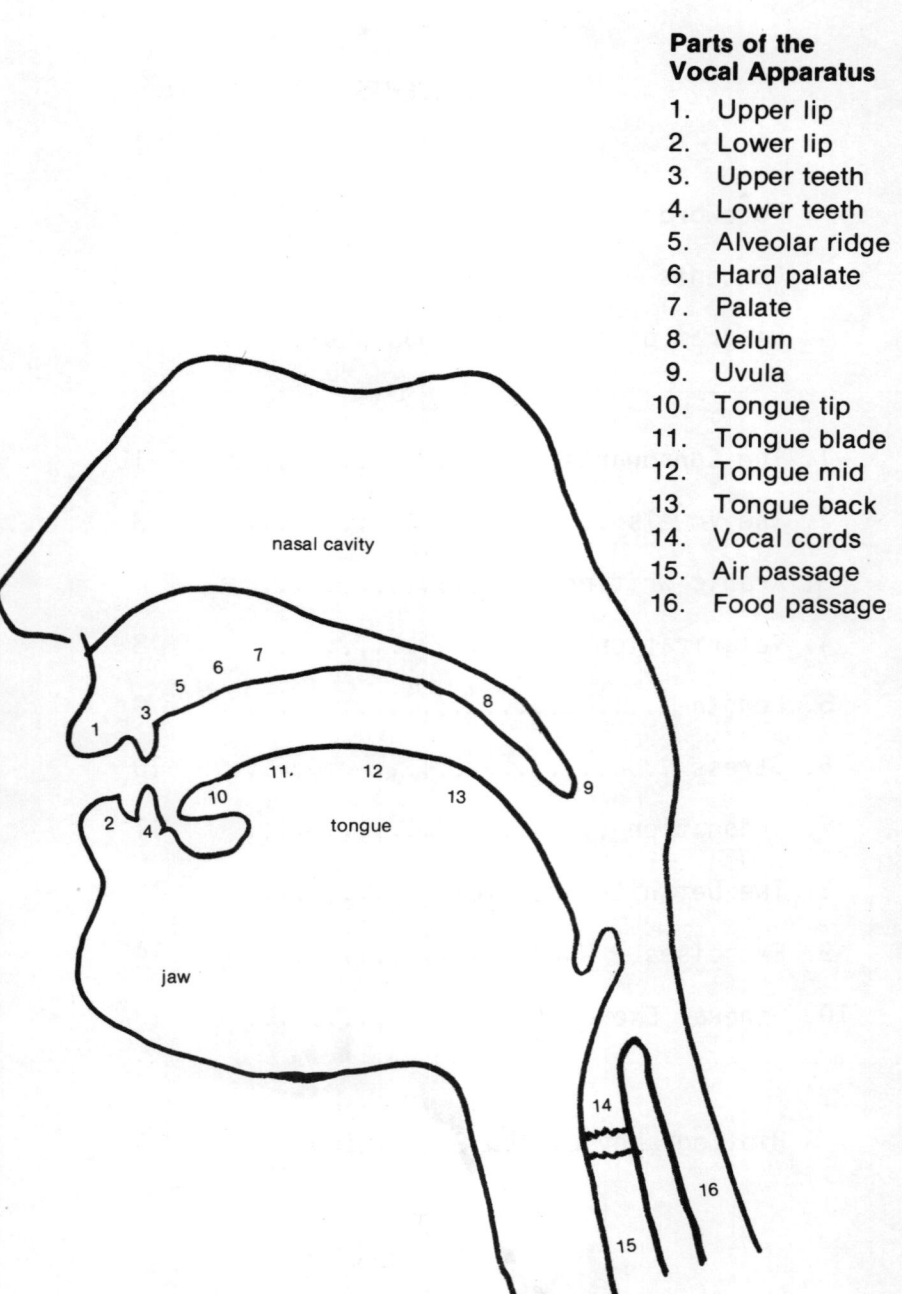

Parts of the Vocal Apparatus
1. Upper lip
2. Lower lip
3. Upper teeth
4. Lower teeth
5. Alveolar ridge
6. Hard palate
7. Palate
8. Velum
9. Uvula
10. Tongue tip
11. Tongue blade
12. Tongue mid
13. Tongue back
14. Vocal cords
15. Air passage
16. Food passage

1. THE CONSONANTS

There are twenty-eight letters in the Arabic alphabet.[1] They are:

Letter	Phonemic transcription and English examples		Name	Description
ا	ʔ		ʔalif	Voiceless glottal stop.
ب	b	**bit**	baa	Voiced bilabial stop.
ت	t	**tea**	taa	Voiceless dental stop.
ث	Θ	**th**in	Θaa	Voiceless interdental fricative.
ج	ž	mea**s**ure	žiim	Voiced alveopalatal fricative.
ح	ħ		ħaa	Voiceless pharyngeal fricative.
خ	x		xaa	Voiceless velar fricative.
د	d	**do**	daal	Voiced dental stop.
ذ	ð	**then**	ðaal	Voiced interdental fricative.
ر	r	**row**	raa	Voiced alveolar flap.
ز	z	**zoo**	zayn	Voiced alveolar fricative.
س	s	**so**	siin	Voiceless alveolar fricative.
ش	š	**she**	šiin	Voiceless alveopalatal fricative.
ص	S		SaaD	Voiceless alveolar velarized fricative.

---

1. /w/ and /y/ are here considered as consonants. They may also be considered as vowels, /ii/ and /uu/. /aa/ is often not included in the alphabet.

Letter	Phonemic transcription and English examples	Name	Description
ض	D	DaaD	Voiced dental velarized stop.
ط	T	Tah	Voiceless dental velarized stop.
ظ	Ð	Ðah	Voiced velarized interdental fricative.
ع	9	9ayn	Voiced pharyngeal fricative.
غ	g	gayn	Voiced velar fricative.
ف	f	**f**un	faa	Voiceless labio-dental fricative.
ق	q		qaaf	Voiceless pharyngeal stop.
ك	k	**c**ook	kaaf	Voiceless velar stop.
ل	l	**l**ow	laam	Voiced alveolar lateral.
م	m	**m**y	miim	Voiced bilabial nasal.
ن	n	**n**o	nuun	Voiced alveolar nasal.
ه	h	**h**igh	haa	Voiceless glottal fricative.
و	w	**w**et	waaw	Voiced bilabial continuant.
ي	y	**y**et	yaa	Voiced palatal continuant.

2. THE VOWELS

There are six vowels in Arabic: three long ones, which appear (except, sometimes, for one) in the alphabet; and three short ones, which do not appear in the alphabet but which are sometimes used in printed texts. Such texts are called voweled texts.

2.1 The Long Vowels

    a. /aa/ pronounced like the **a** in **cat**, unless it is contiguous to a velarized consonant, in which case it is pronounced like the **a** in **car**. (The velarized consonants are symbolized by capital letters.)
    b. /uu/ prounounced like the **oo** in **pool**.
    c. /ii/ pronounced like the **ee** in **meet**, unless it is contiguous to a velarized consonant, in which case it is velarized (backed) too.

2.2 The Short Vowels

    a. /a/ pronounced like the **a** in **cat** (only much shorter), unless it is contiguous to a velarized consonant, in which case it is pronounced like the **u** in **but**.
    b. /u/ pronounced like the **u** in **put**.
    c. /i/ pronounced like the **i** in **bit**, unless it is contiguous to a velarized consonant, in which case it is velarized (backed) too.

2.3 Diphthongs

There are two dipthongs in Arabic:
    a. /aw/ which is a combination of /a/ and /w/ (or /u/).
    b. /ay/ which is a combination of /a/ and /y/ (or /i/).

Note: The following endings are sometimes used, depending on grammatical elements:
        (˝) /un/ for the nominative case.
        (˝) or (΍˝) /an/ generally for the accusative case.
        (̦) /in/ generally for the genitive case.

3. ARABIC WRITING

Arabic writing goes from right to left; and, although words are separated from each other by spaces, yet not all the letters in each word are necessarily attachable to each other. Some letters are attachable only to letters preceding them; some are attachable to letters following them; and some are attachable to both.

Following are the different forms of each letter according to its position (initial, medial, or final) in a word:

EXERCISE ONE:
Look, Listen and **Repeat**

إ أ ﺂ	/ʔaʔuʔi/	أنا	/ʔana/	"I"
		أَنْبَاءٌ	/ʔanbaaʔun/	"news"
		سَأَلَ	/saʔala/	"he asked"
بَبُبِ	/babubi/	بَابٌ	/baabun/	"door"
		سَبَبٌ	/sababun/	"cause"
تَتُتِ	/tatuti/[1]	تُوتٌ	/tuutun/[2]	"mulberry"
		كَتَبَ	/kataba/	"he wrote"
ثَثُثِ	/θaθuθi/	ثُلْثٌ	/θulθun/	"one third"
		مَثَلٌ	/maθalun/	"example"
جَجُجِ	/žažuži/	دَجَاجٌ	/dažaažun/	"chickens"
		رَجُلٌ	/ražulun/	"man"

---

1. Final feminine singular /t/ is written in two ways:
   ﺔ when it is attached, and ة when it is not attached.

2. The small zero sign (°) above a letter means that the letter is not followed by a vowel.

1

		جَاءَ	/žaa?a/ "he came"
حَحُحِ	/ḥaḥuḥi/	إلْحَاحٌ	/?ilḥaaḥun/ "insistence"
		حُوْتٌ	/ḥuutun/ "whale"
خَخُخِ	/xaxuxi/	خَوْخٌ	/xawxun/ "plums"
		نَخْلٌ	/naxlun/ "palms"
دَ دُ دِ	/dadudi/	دُوْدٌ	/duudun/ "worms"
		مَدَّ	/madda/[1] "he extended"
ذَ ذُ ذِ	/ðaðuði/	ذَهَبَ	/ðahaba/ "he went"
		سَيَذْهَبُ	/sayaðhabu/ "he will go"
		رَذَاذٌ	/raðaaðun/ "drizzle"
رَ رُ رِ	/raruri/	رَنَّ	/ranna/ "he rang"
		كَرَّرَ	/karrara/ "he repeated"
زَ زُ زِ	/zazuzi/	كَرَزٌ	/karazun/ "cherries"
		زِرٌّ	/zirrun/ "button"
		مُزَيَّنٌ	/muzayyanun/ "decorated"
سَسُسِ	/sasusi/	سُوْسٌ	/suusun/ "licorice"

---

1. The small w sign (ّ) above a letter means that the letter is geminated (doubled).

1

		مَسَاءٌ	/masaa?un/ "evening"
شَشُبِش	/šašuši/	مِشْمِشٌ	/mišmišun/ "apricots"
		شَمْسٌ	/šamsun/ "sun"
صَصُصِ	/SaSuSi/	صَارَ	/SaaRa/ "he became"
		لُصُوصٌ	/LuSuuSun/ "thieves"
ضَضُضِ	/DaDuDi/	أَرْضٌ	/?aRDun/ "land"
		ضَبَابٌ	/Dabaabun/ "fog"
		قَضِيبٌ	/qaDiibun/ "stick"
طَطُطِ	/TaTuTi/	طَارَ	/TaaRa/ "he flew"
		خُطُوطٌ	/xuTuuTun/ "lines"
ظَظُظِ	/ÐaÐuÐi/	حَظٌّ	/haÐÐun/ "luck"
		ظَنَّ	/Ðanna/ "he thought"
		مُظْلِمٌ	/muÐLimun/ "dark"
عَعُعِ	/9a9u9i/	نَعْنَاعٌ	/na9naa9un/ "mint"
		عَلَى	/9ala/ "on"
غَغُغِ	/gagugi/	غَسَّلَ	/gassala/ "he washed"
		بَلَاغٌ[1]	/balaagun/ "bulletin"
		مُغَنٍّ	/mugannin/ "singer"
فَفُفِ	/fafufi/	فِلْفِلٌ	/filfilun/ "pepper"
		أَلْفٌ	/?alfun/ "thousand"

1. /laa/ is written لا

1

قَقُقِ	/qaquqi/	قَلِقَ	/qaliqa/ "he worried"
		نَقَلْتُ	/naqaltu/ "I moved"
كَكُكِ	/kakuki/	كَعْكٌ	/ka9kun/ "cake"
		سَكَنَتْ	/sakanat/ "she resided"
لَلُلِ	/laluli/	لَيْلٌ	/laylun/ "night"
		بَلَدٌ	/baladun/ "town"
مَمُمِ	/mamumi/	أَمَامَ	/ʔamaama/ "in front of"
		سَمِعْتُ	/sami9tu/ "I heard"
نَنُنِ	/nanuni/	نُونٌ	/nuunun/ "n"
		مِنّا	/minna/ "from us"
هَهُهِ	/hahuhi/[1]	هُنَا	/huna/ "here"
		كِتَابُهُ	/kitaabuhu/ "his book"
		كِتَابُها	/kitaabuha/ "her book"
		سَمَاؤُهُ	/samaaʔuhu/ "his sky"
وَوُوِ	/wawuwi/	وَلْوَلَ	/walwala/ "he moaned"
		سَوَادٌ	/sawaadun/ "blackness"
		لَوْ	/law/ "if"
يَيُيِ	/yayuyi/[2]	يَمْشِي	/yamši/ "he walks"
		سَيِّدٌ	/sayyidun/ "master"

1. Final /h/ is written in two ways: ‍ه when it is attached and ه when it is not attached.
2. The mark for a doubled letter followed by /i/ is either ّ as in سَيِّدٌ or ِّ as in سَيِّدٌ.

4. VELARIZATION[1]

Velarization is a phonological feature in Arabic which presents some problems to foreigners. The velarized consonants of the alphabet are:

/S/ as in	صَارَ	"he became"
/D/ as in	ضَرَبَ	"he hit"
/T/ as in	طَارَ	"he flew"
/Ð/ as in	ظَلامٌ	"darkness"

However, in Arabic speech there are two more velarized consonants, which do not appear as separate letters in the alphabet:

/L/ as in	أَللهُ	"God"
/R/ as in	رَاحَ	"he went"

The important thing to remember about velarization is that a velarized consonant tends to velarize the rest of the word in which it occurs. For example,

إسْتَطَاعَ "he was able" is actually

pronounced إصْطَطَاعَ with velarized vowels.

---

1. See also Section 9.3.

5. LENGTH (GEMINATION)

By length is meant the duration of time in which a sound is produced. This does **not** mean the **speed** at which a person speaks. It means the **relative** length of time in which each separate sound is produced, as compared with a longer or shorter time in which the same or other sounds may be produced in the stream of speech.

Length in Arabic is phonemic. This means that variations in the length of consonants and vowels produce variations in meaning. The difference between the short (single) and long (geminated) sounds is that the long sounds take a relatively longer time to be completely produced than the short ones. In the case of a stop, the explosion comes after a longer withholding; in the case of a fricative, it is continued longer; in the case of a flap, the flaps are repeated (hence the trills); in the case of a nasal, the vibration of the vocal cords and the flow of breath through the nasal passage last longer.

Examples:

Stop.   مَدَى   /mada/ "extent"

مَدَّ   /madda/ "he stretched"

Fricative.   مَسَاؤُهُ   /masaaʔuhu/ "his evening"

مَسَّاهُ   /massaahu/ "he said 'Good evening' to him"

Flap.   بَرَى   /bara/ "he sharpened"

بَرَّأَ   /barraʔa/ "he acquitted"

Nasal.   سَماؤُهُ   /samaaʔuhu/ "his sky"

سَمَّاهُ   /sammaahu/ "he named him"

6. STRESS

By stress is meant the relative force of breath with which sounds are produced. There are three stress levels in Arabic:
   a. primary stress, symbolized by / ´ /
   b. secondary stress, symbolized by / ` /
   c. tertiary (weak) stress, symbolized by no mark.

The occurrence of these three stress levels is predictable, depending on the syllabic[1] formation of words:

a. If a word consists of one short syllable, it takes a primary stress. For example: /mín/ "from"; /lám/ "not"

b. If a word consists of two or three short syllables, the first syllable takes a primary stress and the rest take weak stresses. For example: /ʔána/ "I"; /ʔábadan/ "not at all".

c. If a word consists of one long syllable, it takes a primary stress. For example: /TáaR/ "he flew"; /šáRT/ "bet".

d. If a word consists of two or three long syllables, the last syllable takes a primary stress and the rest take secondary stresses. For example: /TàawúuS/ "peacock"; /sìzzàadáat/ "carpets".

e. If a word consists of four syllables, the primary stress falls on the second syllable, unless the third or fourth syllable is long. Any other long syllable in the word takes secondary stress, and any other short syllable takes a weak stress. For example: /màdrásatun/ "school"; /ʔakalúuha/ "they ate it".

f. If a word consists of five syllables, the third syllable takes a primary stress. All other long syllables take secondary stresses, and all other short syllables take weak stresses. For example: /ʔìhtimáamuhu/ "his interest"; /màdrasátuna/ "our school".

In addition to word stresses, there is a sentence stress which is moveable according to the meaning or meanings the speaker wishes to elicit.
For example:

---

1. Syllables are either short or long. A long syllable is one that contains a long vowel and/or a consonant cluster. A short syllable is one that contains a single vowel followed either by nothing or by a single consonant.

هذا كِتابُهُ /háaða kitáabuhu/ "This (not that) is his book."

هذا كَتابُهُ /háaða katáabuhu/ "This is his book (not notebook, etc.)"

7. INTONATION

By intonation is meant the relative pitch of the voice while producing sounds. In Arabic there are four relative pitch levels which add meaning to an utterance as two or three levels combine to form intonational glides or contours. Wherever there is a primary stress, there is a new contour, and it is the frequent number of primary stresses and intonational contours that gives rise to the staccato rhythm in Arabic. Different contours give different additional meanings.
For example:

هُوَ طَبِيبٌ /huwa Tabiibun/ with falling intonation

at the end is a statement (He is a doctor.)

and with rising intonation at the end is a

question (He is a doctor?)

8. THE DEFINITE ARTICLE

The definite article ٱلْ /ʔal/ is pronounced before the following sounds:[1]

EXERCISE TWO: Look, Listen, and Repeat

ʔ	أَلْأَكْلُ	/ʔalʔaklu/ "the food"
b	أَلْبابُ	/ʔalbaabu/ "the door"
ž	أَلْجَمَلُ	/ʔalžamalu/ "the camel"
ḥ	أَلْحُوْتُ	/ʔalḥuutu/ "the whale"
x	أَلْخَرُوْفُ	/ʔalxaruufu/ "the sheep"
9	أَلْعَيْنُ	/ʔal9aynu/ "the eye"
g	أَلْغَيْمُ	/ʔalgaymu/ "the clouds"
f	أَلْفِيْلُ	/ʔalfiilu/ "the elephant"
q	أَلْقِرْدُ	/ʔalqirdu/ "the monkey"
k	أَلْكِيْسُ	/ʔalkiisu/ "the bag"
m	أَلْماءُ	/ʔalmaaʔu/ "the water"
h	أَلْهَوَاءُ	/ʔalhawaaʔu/ "the air"
w	أَلْوَرْدُ	/ʔalwardu/ "the roses"
y	أَلْيَدُ	/ʔalyadu/ "the hand"

---

1. Here, when a word containing the definite article is preceded by a vowel, only the /l/ of the article is pronounced. For example: مِنَ ٱلْمَدْرَسَةِ /mina lmadrasati/ "from the school". In such a case, the first letter of the article is written: ٱ

The definite article (specifically, the /l/) is not pronounced before the following sounds:[1] (instead, the first sound in the word is doubled).

EXERCISE THREE: Look, Listen, and Repeat

t	أَلتَّاجُ	/ʔattaažu/	"the crown"
θ	أَلثَّلْجُ	/ʔaθθalžu/	"the snow"
d	أَلدَّفْتَرُ	/ʔaddaftaru/	"the notebook"
ð	أَلذَّرَّةُ	/ʔaððarratu/	"the atom"
r	أَلرَّأْسُ	/ʔarraʔsu/	"the head"
z	أَلزَّيْتُ	/ʔazzaytu/	"the oil"
s	أَلسَّمَاءُ	/ʔassamaaʔu/	"the sky"
š	أَلشَّمْسُ	/ʔaššamsu/	"the sun"
S	أَلصَّدَى	/ʔaSSaDa/	"the echo"
D	أَلضَّبَابُ	/ʔaDDabaabu/	"the fog"
T	أَلطَّيْرُ	/ʔaTTayru/	"the bird"
Ð	أَلظَّهْرُ	/ʔaÐÐahru/	"the back"
l	أَللَّيْلُ	/ʔallaylu/	"the night"
n	أَلنَّاسُ	/ʔannaasu/	"the people"

1. Here, when a word containing the definite article is preceded by a vowel, all the letters of the article are not pronounced For example: مِنَ ٱلنَّاسِ /mina nnaasi/ "from the people". Here also, the first letter of the article is written: ٱ .

9. EXERCISES: WORDS

The exercises in reading words are arranged in order of least difficulty to native speakers of English.

9.1   w   y   n   m   h   k   f   s   š   z   ð   Θ   b

These sounds are practically the same as their English equivalents.

EXERCISE FOUR: Look, Listen, and Repeat

فَهِمَ	/fahima/ "he understood"
ذَنَبٌ	/ðanabun/ "tail"
شَوَى	/šawa/ "he barbecued"
سَكَنَ	/sakana/ "he lived"
هَزَّ	/hazza/ "he shook"
وَثَبَ	/waΘaba/ "he jumped"
سَكَبَ	/sakaba/ "he poured"
كِيسٌ	/kiisun/ "bag"
سَاهَمَ	/saahama/ "he participated"
كَشَفَ	/kašafa/ "he uncovered"

9.2 l r d ž t ʔ

These sounds present phonetic problems to native speakers of English; that is, although the sounds occur in English, they either are articulated differently in Arabic, or have a different distribution.

/t/ and /d/ are dental rather than alveolar. In pronouncing these sounds, let your tongue tip touch the back of your upper teeth.

/ž/ and /ʔ/ occur in word initial, medial, and final positions.

/r/ is flapped when it is single and trilled when it is doubled.

/l/ is much lighter than English /l/ except in the word "God" (الله) and when it is contiguous to velarized consonants.

EXERCISE FIVE: Look, Listen, and Repeat

إجْتِهادٌ	/ʔižtihaadun/ "endeavor"
رَجُلٌ	/ražulun/ "man"
رِجْلٌ	/rižlun/ "leg"
سَأَلَ	/saʔala/ "he asked"
مَساءٌ	/masaaʔun/ "evening"
سُؤَالٌ	/suʔaalun/ "question"
جَوَابٌ	/žawaabun/ "answer"
تُوتٌ	/tuutun/ "mulberry"
دُودَةٌ	/duudatun/ "worm"
دَجَاجَةٌ	/dažaažatun/ "chicken"

9.3 Ð T D S

These are the four velarized consonants in the alphabet that tend to velarize other consonants and vowels contiguous to them. One point of departure for English speakers may be the difference in the **t**'s, **d**'s, and **s**'s in the following English words:

till	**t**all
did	**d**oll
sill	**S**aul

The initial consonants in the second column are somewhat backed in comparison with the initial consonants in the first column. This, of course, is due to the vowel qualities in the words, but the distinction there (which has to be magnified in Arabic) may serve as a starting point.

EXERCISE SIX: **Look, Listen, and Repeat**

صَيَّادٌ	/SayyaaDun/	"hunter"
ضَرَبَ	/DaRaba/	"he hit"
طَارَ	/TaaRa/	"he flew"
ظَلامٌ	/Ðalaamun/	"darkness"
سَيَضْرِبُ	/sayaDRibu/	"he is going to hit"
صَارَ	/SaaRa/	"he became"
مَطَرٌ	/maTaRun/	"rain"
ظَبْيٌ	/Ðabyun/	"gazelle"
مَصْيَفٌ	/maSyafun/	"summer resort"
مَضَى	/maDa/	"he passed"

9.4 q g 9 x ḥ

These are the most difficult Arabic sounds for English speakers; and they can be best learned by mimicking native informants.

EXERCISE SEVEN: Look, Listen, and Repeat

حَرْفٌ	/ḥarfun/ "letter"
خَرُوفٌ	/xaruufun/ "sheep"
عَلَى	/9ala/ "on"
غَابَةٌ	/gaabatun/ "forest"
قَالَ	/qaala/ "he said"
حَلْقَةٌ	/ḥalqatun/ "ring"
غُلامٌ	/gulaamun/ "boy"
قَاعِدَةٌ	/qaa9idatun/ "base"
سَامَحَ	/saamaḥa/ "he forgave"
يَخْتَلِفُ	/yaxtalifu/ "he differs"

10. GENERAL EXERCISES

EXERCISE EIGHT:
The Numbers 1—10 (with masculine nouns)

Look, Listen, and Repeat

1. One : God is one. ١ . وَاحِدٌ : أَللهُ وَاحِدٌ .

2. Two : I have two pencils. ٢ . إِثْنَانِ : عِنْدِي قَلَمَانِ اثْنَانِ .

3. Three : I bought three books. ٣ . ثَلاَثَةٌ : إِشْتَرَيْتُ ثَلاَثَةَ كُتُبٍ .

4. Four : He has four children. ٤ . أَرْبَعَةٌ : لَهُ أَرْبَعَةُ أَوْلاَدٍ .

5. Five : He opened five doors. ٥ . خَمْسَةٌ : فَتَحَ خَمْسَةَ أَبْوَابٍ .

6. Six : He took six men with him. ٦ . سِتَّةٌ : أَخَذَ سِتَّةَ رِجَالٍ مَعَهُ .

7. Seven : I read seven books. ٧ . سَبْعَةٌ : قَرَأْتُ سَبْعَةَ كُتُبٍ .

8. Eight : He bought eight notebooks. ٨ . ثَمَانِيَةٌ : إِشْترى ثَمَانِيَةَ دَفَاتِرٍ .

9. Nine : He painted nine walls. ٩ . تِسْعَةٌ : دَهَنَ تِسْعَةَ حِيْطَانٍ .

10. Ten : I observed ten children. ١٠ . عَشَرَةٌ : رَاقَبْتُ عَشَرَةَ أَطْفَالٍ .

You have probably noticed that the numbers 1 and 2 are masculine with masculine nouns. The numbers 3 to 10, however, are feminine with masculine nouns. The opposite is true with feminine nouns.

EXERCISE NINE:
The Numbers 1—10 (with feminine nouns)

Look, Listen, and Repeat

1. One : I read one magazine. ١ . وَاحِدَةٌ : قَرَأْتُ مَجَلَّةً وَاحِدَةً .

2. Two : He has two sisters. ٢ . إِثْنَتَانِ : لَهُ أُخْتَانِ اثْنَتَانِ .

3. Three : He stayed here three hours. ٣ . ثَلَاثٌ : بَقِيَ هُنَا ثَلَاثَ سَاعَاتٍ .

4. Four : I wrote four words. ٤ . أَرْبَعٌ : كَتَبْتُ أَرْبَعَ كَلِمَاتٍ .

5. Five : Five ladies arrived. ٥ . خَمْسٌ : وَصَلَتْ خَمْسُ سَيِّدَاتٍ .

6. Six : Six planes flew. ٦ . سِتٌّ : طَارَتْ سِتُّ طَائِرَاتٍ .

7. Seven : Seven girls entered. ٧ . سَبْعٌ : دَخَلَتْ سَبْعُ فَتَيَاتٍ .

8. Eight : He has eight sisters. ٨ . ثَمَانٍ : لَهُ ثَمَانِي أَخَوَاتٍ .

9. Nine : He bought nine newspapers. ٩ . تِسْعٌ : إِشْتَرَى تِسْعَ جَرَائِدَ .

10. Ten : He is ten years old. ١٠ . عَشْرٌ : عُمْرُهُ عَشْرُ سَنَوَاتٍ .

EXERCISE TEN:
The Days of the Week

Look, Listen, and Repeat

1. Monday. Today is Monday.
   He arrived on Monday.

   ١ . ألإثْنَيْنِ : أَلْيَوْمُ يَوْمُ ٱلإثْنَيْنِ .
   وَصَلَ يَوْمَ ٱلإثْنَيْنِ .

2. Tuesday. Today is Tuesday.
   She arrived on Tuesday.

   ٢ . ألثُّلاثَاءُ : أَلْيَوْمُ يَوْمُ ٱلثُّلاثَاءِ .
   وَصَلَتْ يَوْمَ ٱلثُّلاثَاءِ .

3. Wednesday. Today is Wednesday. I arrived on Wednesday.

   ٣ . ألأربِعاءُ : أَلْيَوْمُ يَوْمُ ٱلأربِعاءِ .
   وَصَلْتُ يَوْمَ ٱلأربِعاءِ .

4. Thursday. Today is Thursday.
   We arrived on Thursday.

   ٤ . ألْخَمِيسُ : أَلْيَوْمُ يَوْمُ ٱلْخَمِيسِ .
   وَصَلْنا يَوْمَ ٱلْخَمِيسِ .

5. Friday. Today is Friday.
   You (masculine, singular) arrived on Friday.

   ٥ . ألْجُمُعَةُ : أَلْيَوْمُ يَوْمُ ٱلْجُمُعَةِ .
   وَصَلْتَ يَوْمَ ٱلْجُمُعَةِ .

6. Saturday. Today is Saturday.
   They (masculine) arrived on Saturday.

   ٦ . ألسَّبْتُ : أَلْيَوْمُ يَوْمُ ٱلسَّبْتِ .
   وَصَلُوا يَوْمَ ٱلسَّبْتِ .

7. Sunday. Today is Sunday.
   They (feminine) arrived on Sunday.

   ٧ . ألأحَدُ : أَلْيَوْمُ يَوْمُ ٱلأحَدِ .
   وَصَلْنَ يَوْمَ ٱلأحَدِ .

EXERCISE ELEVEN:
The Months of the Year

Look, Listen, and Repeat

1. January. In January. ١ . كَانُوْنُ ٱلثَّانِي : فِي كَانُوْنَ ٱلثَّانِي .

2. February. The month of February. ٢ . شُبَاطُ : شَهْرُ شُبَاط .

3. March. In the month of March. ٣ . آذَارُ : فِي شَهْرِ آذَار .

4. April. During the month of April. ٤ . نَيْسَانُ : خِلَالَ شَهْرِ نَيْسَان .

5. May. Before the month of May. ٥ . أَيَّارُ : قَبْلَ شَهْرِ أَيَّار .

6. June. After the month of June. ٦ . حُزَيْرَانُ : بَعْدَ شَهْرِ حُزَيْرَان .

7. July. On the fifth of July. ٧ . تَمُّوْزُ : فِي ٱلخَامِسِ مِن تَمُّوْز .

8. August. All the month of August. ٨ . آبُ : كُلُّ شَهْرِ آب .

9. September. In the beginning of September. ٩ . أَيْلُوْلُ : فِي أَوَائِلِ أَيْلُوْل .

10. October. In the middle of October. ١٠ . تِشْرِيْنُ ٱلأَوَّلُ : فِي نِصفِ تِشْرِيْنَ ٱلأَوَّل

11. November. On the second of November. ١١ . تِشْرِينُ ٱلثَّانِي : فِي ٱلثَّانِي مِنْ تِشْرِيْنَ ٱلثَّانِي .

12. December. On the twenty-fifth of December. ١٢ . كَانُوْنُ ٱلأَوَّلُ : فِي ٱلخَامِسِ وَٱلْعِشْرِيْنَ مِنْ كَانُوْنَ ٱلأَوَّل .

EXERCISE TWELVE:
The Numbers 20—100 (nominative case)

Look, Listen, and Repeat

1. Twenty : I have twenty books. ١ . عِشْرُوْنَ : عِنْدِي عِشْرُوْنَ كِتَاباً.

2. Thirty : Thirty students came. ٢ . ثَلَاثُوْنَ : جَاءَ ثَلَاثُوْنَ تِلْمِيْذاً.

3. Forty : Forty soldiers went. ٣ . أَرْبَعُوْنَ : ذَهَبَ أَرْبَعُوْنَ جُنْدِيّاً.

4. Fifty : He has fifty dinars. ٤ . خَمْسُوْنَ : عِنْدَهُ خَمْسُوْنَ دِيْناراً.

5. Sixty : Sixty ladies came. ٥ . سِتُّوْنَ : أَتَتْ سِتُّوْنَ سَيِّدَةً.

6. Seventy : Seventy cables arrived. ٦ . سَبْعُوْنَ : وَصَلَتْ سَبْعُوْنَ بَرقِيَّةً.

7. Eighty : Eighty persons were present. ٧ . ثَمانُوْنَ : حَضَرَ ثَمانُوْنَ شَخْصاً.

8. Ninety : Ninety questions were asked. ٨ . تِسْعُوْنَ : سُئِلَ تِسْعُوْنَ سُؤَالاً.

9. One hundred : He has one hundred papers. ٩ . مِئَةٌ : لَدَيْهِ مِئَةُ وَرَقَةٍ.

EXERCISE THIRTEEN:
The Numbers 20—100 (accusative case)

Look, Listen, and Repeat

1. Twenty : I read twenty books.

١ . عِشْرِيْنَ : قَرَأْتُ عِشْرِيْنَ كِتاباً .

2. Thirty : He taught thirty students.

٢ . ثَلاثيْنَ : عَلَّمَ ثَلاثيْنَ تِلْمِيْذاً .

3. Forty : He bought forty loaves.

٣ . أَرْبَعِيْنَ : إشْتَرَى أَرْبَعِيْنَ رَغيْفاً .

4. Fifty : She gave me fifty notebooks.

٤ . خَمْسِيْنَ : أَعْطَتْني خَمْسِيْنَ دَفْتَراً .

5. Sixty : He asked sixty questions.

٥ . سِتِّيْنَ : سَأَلَ سِتِّيْنَ سُؤالاً .

6. Seventy : He sent seventy cables.

٦ . سَبْعِيْنَ : أَرْسَلَ سَبْعِيْنَ بَرْقِيَّةً .

7. Eighty : She threw eighty balls.

٧ . ثَمانِيْنَ : رَمَتْ ثَمانِيْنَ كُرَةً .

8. Ninety : He lived ninety years.

٨ . تِسْعِيْنَ : عاشَ تِسْعِيْنَ سَنَةً .

9. One hundred : He requested one hundred trees.

٩ . مِئَةً : طَلَبَ مِئَةَ شَجَرَةٍ .

EXERCISE FOURTEEN:
Nominal Sentences

Look, Listen, and Repeat

1.	The sun is strong.	١ . اَلشَّمْسُ قَوِيَّةٌ .
2.	The moon is beautiful.	٢ . اَلْقَمَرُ جَمِيلٌ .
3.	This man is strong.	٣ . هَذا الرَّجُلُ قَوِيٌّ .
4.	The children are in school.	٤ . اَلأَوْلادُ في الْمَدْرَسَةِ .
5.	The gift is precious.	٥ . اَلْهَدِيَّةُ ثَمِينَةٌ .
6.	The paper is thin.	٦ . اَلْوَرَقُ رَقِيقٌ .
7.	The book is expensive.	٧ . اَلْكِتابُ غَالٍ .
8.	The story is long.	٨ . اَلْقِصَّةُ طَوِيلَةٌ .
9.	The weather is cold.	٩ . اَلطَّقْسُ بارِدٌ .
10.	The dog is a loyal animal.	١٠ . اَلْكَلْبُ حَيَوانٌ أَمِينٌ .
11.	The parrot is an intelligent bird.	١١ . اَلْبَبْغاءُ عُصْفُورٌ ذَكِيٌّ .
12.	The school is an important institution.	١٢ . اَلْمَدْرَسَةُ مُؤَسَّسَةٌ هامَّةٌ .

EXERCISE FIFTEEN:
Verbal Sentences

Look, Listen, and Repeat

1.	The boy ate an apple.	١ . أَكَلَ ٱلْوَلَدُ تُفَّاحَةً .
2.	The girl drank water.	٢ . شَرِبَتِ ٱلْبِنْتُ ماءً .
3.	The child hit his brother.	٣ . ضَرَبَ ٱلطِّفْلُ أَخاهُ .
4.	The student went to school.	٤ . ذَهَبَ ٱلتِّلْمِيذُ إِلَى ٱلْمَدْرَسَةِ .
5.	He taught me arithmetic.	٥ . عَلَّمَنِي حِساباً .
6.	The man slept in his bed.	٦ . نامَ ٱلرَّجُلُ في فِراشِهِ .
7.	The minister returned from his travels.	٧ . عادَ ٱلْوَزِيرُ مِنْ سَفَرِهِ .
8.	The thief stole the money.	٨ . سَرَقَ ٱللِّصُّ ٱلنُّقُودَ .
9.	The woman washed her clothes.	٩ . غَسَلَتِ ٱلامْرَأَةُ ثِيابَها .
10.	The writer wrote a story.	١٠ . كَتَبَ ٱلْكاتِبُ قِصَّةً .
11.	The poet wrote a poem.	١١ . كَتَبَ ٱلشَّاعِرُ شِعْراً .
12.	I read a long novel.	١٢ . قَرَأْتُ رِوايَةً طَوِيلَةً .

EXERCISE SIXTEEN:
Nominal subjects with verbal predicates

Look, Listen, and Repeat

1.	The boy played in the playground.	١ . اَلْوَلَدُ لَعِبَ في اَلْمَلْعَبِ .
2.	The teacher is teaching his lesson.	٢ . اَلْمُعَلِّمُ يُعَلِّمُ دَرْسَهُ .
3.	The farmers are working in the fields.	٣ . اَلْفَلَّاحُوْنَ يَشْتَغِلُوْنَ في اَلْحُقُوْلِ
4.	The carpenter is doing his work.	٤ . اَلنَّجَّارُ يَعْمَلُ عَمَلَهُ .
5.	The children did not play.	٥ . اَلْأَوْلَادُ لَمْ يَلْعَبُوا .
6.	The maid will not come today.	٦ . اَلْخَادِمَةُ لَنْ تَحْضُرَ اَلْيَوْمَ .
7.	The writer writes.	٧ . اَلْكَاتِبُ يَكْتُبُ .
8.	The parachutist flew high.	٨ . اَلْمِظَلِّيُّ طَارَ عَالِياً .
9.	The man became a specialist.	٩ . اَلرَّجُلُ أَصْبَحَ اَخْتِصَاصِيّاً .
10.	The moon shines.	١٠ . اَلْقَمَرُ يَلْمَعُ .
11.	Over-eating is harmful.	١١ . كَثْرَةُ اَلْأَكْلِ تَضُرُّ .
12.	God loves us.	١٢ . اَللهُ يُحِبُّنَا .

EXERCISE SEVENTEEN:
Miscellaneous sentences

Look, Listen, and Repeat

1. The teacher asked the student a question.

١ . سَأَلَ ٱلْأُسْتَاذُ ٱلتِّلْمِيذَ سُؤَالاً .

2. The man killed the lion with his gun.

٢ . قَتَلَ ٱلرَّجُلُ ٱلْأَسَدَ بِبُنْدُقِيَّتِهِ .

3. The girl is going to go to school tomorrow.

٣ . سَتَذْهَبُ ٱلْبِنْتُ إِلَى ٱلْمَدْرَسَةِ غَداً .

4. This book is larger than mine.

٤ . هَذا ٱلْكِتابُ أَكْبَرُ مِنْ كِتابِي .

5. The woman came home with her daughter.

٥ . أَتَتِ ٱلامْرَأَةُ مَعَ ٱبْنَتِها إِلَى ٱلْبَيْتِ .

6. I lived in Beirut for a period of two years.

٦ . سَكَنْتُ فِي بَيْرُوْتَ مُدَّةَ سَنَتَيْنِ .

7. The thief attempted to steal everything.

٧. حاوَلَ ٱللِّصُّ أَنْ يَسْرِقَ كُلَّ شَيْءٍ .

8. We asked him to repeat the lecture.

٨. طَلَبْنا مِنْهُ إعادَةَ ٱلْمُحاضَرَةِ .

9. I heard the news from the Lebanese broadcasting station.

٩. سَمِعْتُ ٱلْأخْبارَ مِنْ مَحَطَّةِ ٱلْإذاعَةِ ٱللُّبْنانِيَّةِ .

10. They ate bread and drank water.

١٠. أَكَلُوا خُبْزاً وَشَرِبُوا ماءً .

11. He walked towards the sea in the dark.

١١. مَشَى نَحْوَ ٱلْبَحْرِ فِي ٱلظُّلْمَةِ .

12. My father gave me a very beautiful watch.

١٢. أَعْطانِي أَبِي ساعَةً جَمِيلَةً جِدًّا .

EXERCISE EIGHTEEN:
Singular, dual[1], and plural nouns (nominative case)

Look, Listen, and Repeat
(Masculine)

1. Farmer(s)   ١. فَلاَّحٌ – فَلاَّحَانِ – فَلاَّحُوْنَ

2. Carpenter(s)   ٢. نَجَّارٌ – نَجَّارَانِ – نَجَّارُوْنَ

3. Teacher(s)   ٣. مُعَلِّمٌ – مُعَلِّمَانِ – مُعَلِّمُوْنَ

4. Dancer(s)   ٤. رَاقِصٌ – رَاقِصَانِ – رَاقِصُوْنَ

(Feminine)

5. Table(s)   ٥. طَاوِلَةٌ – طَاوِلَتَانِ – طَاوِلاتٌ

6. Word(s)   ٦. كَلِمَةٌ – كَلِمَتَانِ – كَلِمَاتٌ

7. Teacher(s)   ٧. مُعَلِّمَةٌ – مُعَلِّمَتَانِ – مُعَلِّمَاتٌ

8. Dancer(s)   ٨. رَاقِصَةٌ – رَاقِصَتَانِ – رَاقِصَاتٌ

(Broken)

9. Book(s)   ٩. كِتَابٌ – كِتَابَانِ – كُتُبٌ

10. Door(s)   ١٠. بَابٌ – بَابَانِ – أَبْوَابٌ

11. Professor(s)   ١١. أُسْتَاذٌ – أُسْتَاذَانِ – أَسَاتِذَةٌ

12. House(s)   ١٢. بَيْتٌ – بَيْتَانِ – بُيُوتٌ

---

1. The accusative and genitive endings for the dual form are -/ayni/ for the masculine and -/tayni/ for the feminine. Thus: كِتَابٌ : كِتَابَيْنِ

      طَاوِلَةٌ : طَاوِلَتَيْنِ

EXERCISE NINETEEN: Question askers

Look, Listen, and Repeat

1. Who came?
   Who went?

   ١. مَنْ جَاءَ؟
   مَنْ ذَهَبَ؟

2. What is the question?
   What is your opinion?

   ٢. ما ٱلسُّؤالُ؟
   ما رَأْيُكَ؟

3. What did he read?
   What does he want?

   ٣. ماذا قَرَأَ؟
   ماذا يُرِيدُ؟

4. How did he travel?
   How are you?

   ٤. كَيْفَ سافَرَ؟
   كَيْفَ حالُكَ؟

5. When did he arrive?
   When did she sleep?

   ٥. مَتَى وَصَلَ؟
   مَتَى نامَتْ؟

6. Where did they go?
   Where did he live?

   ٦. أَيْنَ ذَهَبُوا؟
   أَيْنَ سَكَنَ؟

7. Why did he fly to us?
   Why did he say what he said?

   ٧. لِماذا طارَ إلَيْنا؟
   لِماذا قالَ ما قالَ؟

8. Did the professor come?
   Did she study her lessons?

   ٨. هَلْ أَتَى ٱلأُسْتاذُ؟
   هَلْ دَرَسَتْ دُرُوسَها؟

9. Did the professor come?
   Did she study her lessons?

   ٩. أَأَتَى ٱلأُسْتاذُ؟
   أَدَرَسَتْ دُرُوسَها؟

EXERCISE TWENTY:
Jeha and His Shirt

Look, Listen, and Repeat

جُحا وَقَمِيصُهُ

بَيْنَما كانَ جُحا عائِداً إِلَى بَيْتِهِ ذاتَ يَوْمٍ، إِلْتَقَى بِصَدِيقٍ لَهُ فَسارا مَعاً، وَأَخَذَ كُلٌّ مِنْهُما يَدَّعِي مُتَحَدِّثاً عَنِ ٱلْأَخْطارِ ٱلَّتِي نَجا مِنْها فِي حَياتِهِ.

رَوَى جُحا حِكايَتَهُ عَنْ أَرْبَعَةِ أَخْطارٍ وَقَعَ فِيها وَنَجا مِنْها. وَرَوَى صاحِبُهُ أَرْبَعَ قِصَصٍ مُماثِلَةٍ. وَفَجْأَةً هَبَّتْ عاصِفَةٌ شَدِيدَةٌ، فَطارَ قَمِيصُ جُحا ٱلْمَنْشُورُ عَلَى ٱلسَّطْحِ، وَسَقَطَ فِي مُسْتَنْقَعَةٍ قَرِيبَةٍ مِنْ بَيْتِهِ.

فَصاحَ جُحا: «أَلْحَمْدُ لِلّٰهِ، أَلْحَمْدُ لِلّٰهِ». فَسَأَلَهُ صاحِبُهُ: «لِماذا تَقُولُ ”أَلْحَمْدُ لِلّٰهِ“ وَقَمِيصُكَ فِي تِلْكَ ٱلْمُسْتَنْقَعَةِ ٱلْقَذِرَةِ؟»

فَأَجابَهُ جُحا قائِلاً: «إِنِّي أَشْكُرُ ٱللهَ لِأَنِّي نَجَوْتُ مِنْ خَطَرٍ خامِسٍ، فَلَو كُنْتُ لابِساً ذٰلِكَ ٱلْقَمِيصَ لَحَلَّتْ بِي كارِثَةٌ فَظِيعَةٌ.»

Jeha and His Shirt

As Jeha was returning home one day, he met a friend of his, and they walked together. Each one of them boasted about the dangers he had escaped from in his life.

Jeha told his story about four dangers he fell in and escaped from. And his friend related four similar stories. Suddenly a strong storm blew and Jeha's shirt that was hanging on the roof flew and fell into a puddle near his home.

Jeha shouted, "Praise be to God." His friend asked, "Why are you saying, 'Praise be to God' when your shirt is in that dirty puddle?"

Jeha answered saying, "I thank God because I have escaped from a fifth danger, for if I had been wearing that shirt, a terrible catastrophe would have befallen me."

EXERCISE TWENTY-ONE:
Jeha and His Donkey

Look, Listen, and Repeat

جُحا وَحِمارُهُ

كانَ لِجُحا حِمارٌ قَوِيٌّ يَسْتَعْمِلُهُ لِلرُّكُوبِ وَلِلأَحْمالِ الثَّقيلَةِ.
وَكانَ هٰذا الْحِمارُ أَميناً وَوَفِيّاً وَصَبوراً. لا هَمَّ لَهُ في الْحَياةِ
إِلَّا أَنْ يَأْكُلَ أَكْلاً شَهِيّاً. فَإِنْ أَطْعَمَهُ صاحِبُهُ عَمِلَ لَهُ بِكَدٍّ
وَإِخْلاصٍ، وَإِلَّا فَنامَ طولَ النَّهارِ. عَلِمَ جيرانُ جُحا عَنْ هٰذا
الْحِمارِ الْجَيِّدِ، فَكانوا يَأْتونَ إِلَيْهِ طالِبينَ مِنْهُ أَسْتِعْمالَ حِمارِهِ،
وَكانَ جُحا كَريماً مَعَ جيرانِهِ يُقَدِّمُ لَهُمْ حِمارَهُ بِدونِ تَرَدُّدٍ
وَلٰكِنَّهُ كانَ يَطْلُبُ مِنْهُمْ أَنْ يُطْعِموا الْحِمارَ أَكْلاً مُغَذِّياً.

لاحَظَ جُحا بَعْدَ أَيَّامٍ أَنَّ حِمارَهُ كانَ يَعودُ إِلَيْهِ جائِعاً،
فَقَرَّرَ أَلَّا يُعْطي جيرانَهُ الْحِمارَ فيما بَعْدُ.

وَفي يَوْمٍ مِنَ الْأَيَّامِ أَتى أَحَدُ الْجيرانِ إِلَيْهِ وَطَلَبَ الْحِمارَ
فَقالَ لَهُ جُحا: «آسِفْ يا صَديقي، فَإِنَّ حَماري لَيْسَ هُنا، فَلَقَدْ

21   Jeha and His Donkey

ذَهَبَ إِلَى اَلسُّوقِ حامِلاً بِضاعَتي. » وَفي تِلْكَ اَللَّحْظَةِ نَهَقَ اَلْحِمارُ بِصَوْتٍ عالٍ جِدًّا، فَالْتَفَتَ اَلْجارُ نَحْوَ جُحا وَقالَ: «حَسِبْتُكَ جاراً صادِقاً يا جُحا، فَها هُوَ اَلْحِمارُ يَنْهَقُ وَأَنْتَ تَقولُ إِنَّهُ لَيْسَ هُنا.»

فَأَجابَهُ جُحا قائِلاً: «يا عَزيزي، هَلْ تُصَدِّقُ حِماري وَلا تُصَدِّقُ صَديقَكَ؟»

Jeha and His Donkey

Jeha had a strong donkey that he used for riding and for heavy loads. This donkey was loyal and patient, with no worry in life but to eat appetizing food. If his owner fed him, he would work hard and sincerely; otherwise, he would sleep all day.

Jeha's neighbors knew about this good donkey, and they used to come to Jeha asking to use his donkey. Jeha was generous with his neighbors, offering them his donkey without any hesitation. But he used to ask them to feed the donkey nourishing food.

Jeha noticed after some days that his donkey returned to him hungry. So he decided not to give his neighbors the donkey thereafter.

One day one of the neighbors came to him and asked for the donkey. Jeha said to him, "Sorry, my friend, but my donkey is not here. He has gone to the market with my goods." At that moment the donkey brayed very loudly. The neighbor turned to Jeha and said, "I considered you to be an honest neighbor, Jeha. The donkey is braying and you say he is not here."

Jeha answered him saying, "My dear (one), do you believe my donkey and disbelieve your friend?"

EXERCISE TWENTY-TWO
The Immigrants' Visit

Look, Listen, and Repeat
(Attempt a translation)

زِيارَةُ ٱلْمُغْتَرِبين

وَصَلَتْنا رِسالَةٌ لَطيفَةٌ مِنْ إِخْوانِنا ٱلْمُغْتَرِبينَ تُفيدُ أَنَّهُمْ وَصَلوا إِلى بِلادِهِمْ بِخَيْرٍ وَسَلامَةٍ بَعْدَ أَنْ قَضَوْا خَمْسَةَ أَيَّامٍ عَلى مَتْنِ باخِرَةٍ صَغيرَةٍ وَخَفيفَةٍ في بَحْرٍ هائِجٍ تَكادُ أَمْواجُهُ أَنْ تَكونَ جِبالًا شامِخَة .

وَأَضافَ أُولٰئِكَ ٱلْمُغْتَرِبونَ أَنَّ ٱلْأَيَّامَ ٱلَّتي صَرَفوها في لُبْنانَ كانَتْ مِنْ أَجْمَلِ أَيَّامِ حَياتِهِمْ . فَقَدْ تَمَتَّعوا بِهَوائِهِ ٱلطَّلْقِ وَنَسَماتِهِ ٱللَّطيفَةِ وَمَناظِرِهِ ٱلْخَلَّابَةِ وَجِبالِهِ ٱلْخَضْراءِ وَبَحْرِهِ ٱلْأَزْرَقِ وَطَعامِهِ ٱللَّذيذِ ٱلشَّهِيِّ . وَعَبَّروا عَنْ أَمَلِهِمْ بِالرُّجوعِ إِلى رُبوعِ لُبْنانَ في ٱلْمُسْتَقْبَلِ ٱلْقَريبِ ٱلْعاجِلِ .

EXERCISE TWENTY-THREE
Agricultural Concerns

Look, Listen, and Repeat
(Attempt a translation)

شُؤُونٌ زِرَاعِيَّةٌ

يُوَاصِلُ مَجْلِسُ إِدَارَةِ مَكْتَبِ ٱلْفَاكِهَةِ فِي ٱلْجَلْسَةِ ٱلْأُسْبُوعِيَّةِ ٱلَّتِي دُعِيَ لِعَقْدِهَا بَعْدَ ظُهْرِ ٱلْيَوْمِ دَرْسَ ٱلتَّدَابِيرِ ٱلرَّامِيَةِ إِلَى تَشْكِيلِ مَجْلِسِ إِدَارَةِ شَرِكَةِ تَسْوِيقِ ٱلْفَاكِهَةِ وَشَرِكَةِ ٱلْبَوَاخِرِ وَوَضْعِ نِظَامِهَا ٱلدَّاخِلِيِّ .

وَسَيَدْرُسُ مَجْلِسُ ٱلْإِدَارَةِ ٱلتَّدَابِيرَ ٱلَّتِي بَدَأَ بِٱتِّخَاذِهَا عَلَى ٱلصَّعِيدِ ٱلرَّسْمِيِّ لِٱنْتِدَابِ ٱلْفِرَقِ ٱلْإِحْصَائِيَّةِ لِلْٱطِّلَاعِ عَلَى أَوْضَاعِ مَوْسِمِ ٱلْفَاكِهَةِ ٱلْجَدِيدِ فِي مُخْتَلِفِ ٱلْمَنَاطِقِ .

هَذَا ، وَكَانَتْ مَصْلَحَةُ ٱلزِّرَاعَةِ قَدْ عَيَّنَتْ عُمَّالًا لِمُكَافَحَةِ حَشَرَةِ ٱلْمَنِّ ٱلَّتِي تُصِيبُ ٱلْمَحَاصِيلَ ٱلْحَقْلِيَّةَ فِي هَذَا ٱلْفَصْلِ ، وَٱلَّتِي تَنْتَشِرُ بِكَثْرَةٍ فِي مَنَاطِقَ عَدِيدَةٍ .

وَيُؤْخَذُ مِنَ ٱلتَّقَارِيرِ ٱلْوَارِدَةِ إِلَى ٱلْمَصْلَحَةِ أَنَّ أَعْمَالَ

23

ٱلمُكافَحةِ ٱلَّتي قامَ بِها أولئِكَ ٱلعُمّالُ قَدْ أدَّتْ إلى ٱلْقَضاءِ عَلى تِلكَ ٱلحَشَرةِ ٱلْمُؤذيةِ في كَثيرٍ مِنْ مَناطِقِ ٱلجَبَلِ .

وإلى جانِبِ أعمالِ ٱلْمُكافَحةِ باشَرَتِ ٱلْمَصْلَحةُ بِتَوزيعِ ٱلأدويةِ ٱلْمُبيدةِ لِحَشَرةِ ٱلْمَنِّ عَلى ٱلْمُزارِعينَ ٱلَّذينَ أبدَوْا ٱسْتِعداداً لِمُكافَحَتِها بِأنْفُسِهِمْ .

BIBLIOGRAPHY BY THE SAME AUTHOR

(Related to Arabic)

A. BOOKS

1. Colloquial Arabic: an Oral Approach, Librairie du Liban, Beirut, 1966.

2. An English-Colloquial Arabic Dictionary: in Phonetic Script, Librairie du Liban, Beirut, 1972.

3. An Intermediate Colloquial Arabic Course (with Hadia H. Harb), Librairie du Liban, Beirut, 1973.

4. Learn to Read Arabic (with tape), Librairie du Liban, Beirut, 1978.

5. The Structure of Arabic: from Sound to Sentence, Librairie du Liban, Beirut, 1967.

6. The Teaching of Arabic as a Foreign Language, Librairie du Liban, Beirut, 1978.

B. BOOKS IN PREPARATION

1. A Colloquial Arabic-English Dictionary

2. A New English-Arabic Dictionary for Arab Learners

C. ARTICLES

1. "Arabic Vowels and Vocoids: Their Characteristics and Distribution," Proceedings of the Fifth International Congress of Phonetic Sciences, Munster, West Germany, 1964.

2. "Constructive and Destructive Interference in Applied Phonology," <u>Eighth International Congress of Phonetic Sciences</u>, Leeds, England, 1975.

3. "Constructive and Destructive Interference in Applied Phonology II," <u>The Third World Congress of Phoneticians</u>, Tokyo, Japan, 1976.

4. "The Interrelationship of the Supra-Segmental Elements in a Language," <u>World Papers in Phonetic</u> Phonetic Society of Japan, Tokyo, Japan, 1974.

5. "The Morpho-Phonemic Forms of THE in Lebanese Arabic," <u>Anthropological Linguistics</u>, Volume 10, Number 6, June, 1968.

6. "Phonemic Length in Lebanese Arabic," <u>Phonetica</u>, Vol. 5, Nos. 3-4, Basel, Switzerland, 1960.

7. "Phonemic Velarization in Literary Arabic," <u>Proceedings of the Ninth International Congress of Linguists</u>, Cambridge, Massachusetts, 1962.

8. "The Phonetic Environment as the Determiner of the Allomorphic Forms of THE in Standard Arabic," <u>Proceedings of the Seventh International Congress of Phonetic Sciences</u>, Mouton, The Hague, 1972.

9. "The Predictability of Stress in Lebanese Arabic," <u>Phonetica</u>, Vol. 4, Nos. 2-3, Basel, Switzerland, 1959.

10. "The Preparation of Teachers of Arabic as a Foreign Language," (in Arabic), Arabic Language Institute, University of Riyadh, Riyadh, Saudi Arabia, 1978.

11. "Training Criteria for Effective Language Teachers," <u>Transactions of the Fifth AIMAV Seminar</u>, Brussels, Belgium, 1973.

12. "Velarization in Lebanese Arabic," <u>Phonetica</u>, Vol. 3, No. 4, Basel, Switzerland, 1959.